# Gulun'

## Billabong

## About the Indigenous Literacy Foundation

The Indigenous Literacy Foundation (ILF) is a national charity working with Aboriginal and Torres Strait Islander remote Communities across Australia. We are Community-led, responding to requests from remote Communities for culturally relevant books, including early learning board books, resources, and programs to support Communities to create and publish their stories in languages of their choice.

In 2024 the ILF won the Astrid Lindgren Memorial Award, given annually to a person or organisation for their outstanding contribution to kids' or young adult literature.

First published in 2025 by the
Indigenous Literacy Foundation
Gadigal Country
Level 17/207 Kent Street
Sydney NSW 2000
ilf.org.au



Dhuwaya translation by Rärriwuy Gurramu Marika



Cataloguing-in-Publication details are available from the National Library of Australia

www.trove.nla.gov.au

ISBN 9781923179516

Typesetting and design by Lee Burgemeestre
Printed in China by RR Donnelley Asia Printing Solutions Limited

Thanks to ARDS Aboriginal Corporation for translation and logistics support with this project.

ARDS ABORIGINAL CORPORATION
CREATIVE MEDIA & COMMUNICATION SPECIALISTS

# Guḻun'
## Billabong

By children at Yirrkala School

Indigenous Literacy Foundation

# Yol ŋuli nhina gul̲un'ŋuya?

Who lives in the billabong?

1

Waŋgany

# bäru

djäka gurra nhanukalaŋuwu mapuwu.

One crocodile, looking after her eggs.

# 2

Marrma'

muthali'.

Waŋganydja ŋoyŋu gapuŋu!

Two diving ducks. One is under the water!

# 3

Ḻurrkun

# biyay

ŋorra gurra waluŋu.

Three goannas, lying in the sun.

# 4

Ḏambumiriw

## gatapaŋa

l̲upl̲upthun gurra dhol̲uŋu.

Four buffaloes, having a mud bath.

# 5

Waŋgany rulu

## ŋerrk'

buṯthu-buṯthun gurra dharpaŋu.

Five cockatoos, flying through the trees.

Waŋgany rulu ga waŋgany bäythinyaya

**guḏurrku**

giritji gurra galki gapuŋu.

Six brolgas, dancing by the water.

7

Waŋgany rulu ga märrma' bäythinyaya

# minhdharr gark'man

mulka-mulka marrtji ŋula nhä.

Seven green frogs, catching bugs.

# 8

Waŋgany rulu ga l̲urrkun bäythinyaya

**minhala**

djul̲u-djul̲ul̲'yun gurra ŋoyŋu räkayŋu.

Eight long-necked turtles, hiding in the reeds.

# 9

Waŋgany rulu ga d̲ambumiriw

## d̲akawa

l̲irra' raywalmi. Yaaakay!

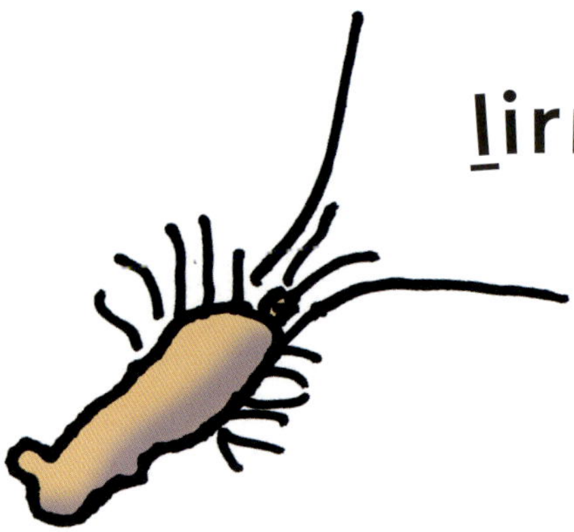

Nine yabbies, with sharp nippers. Ouch!

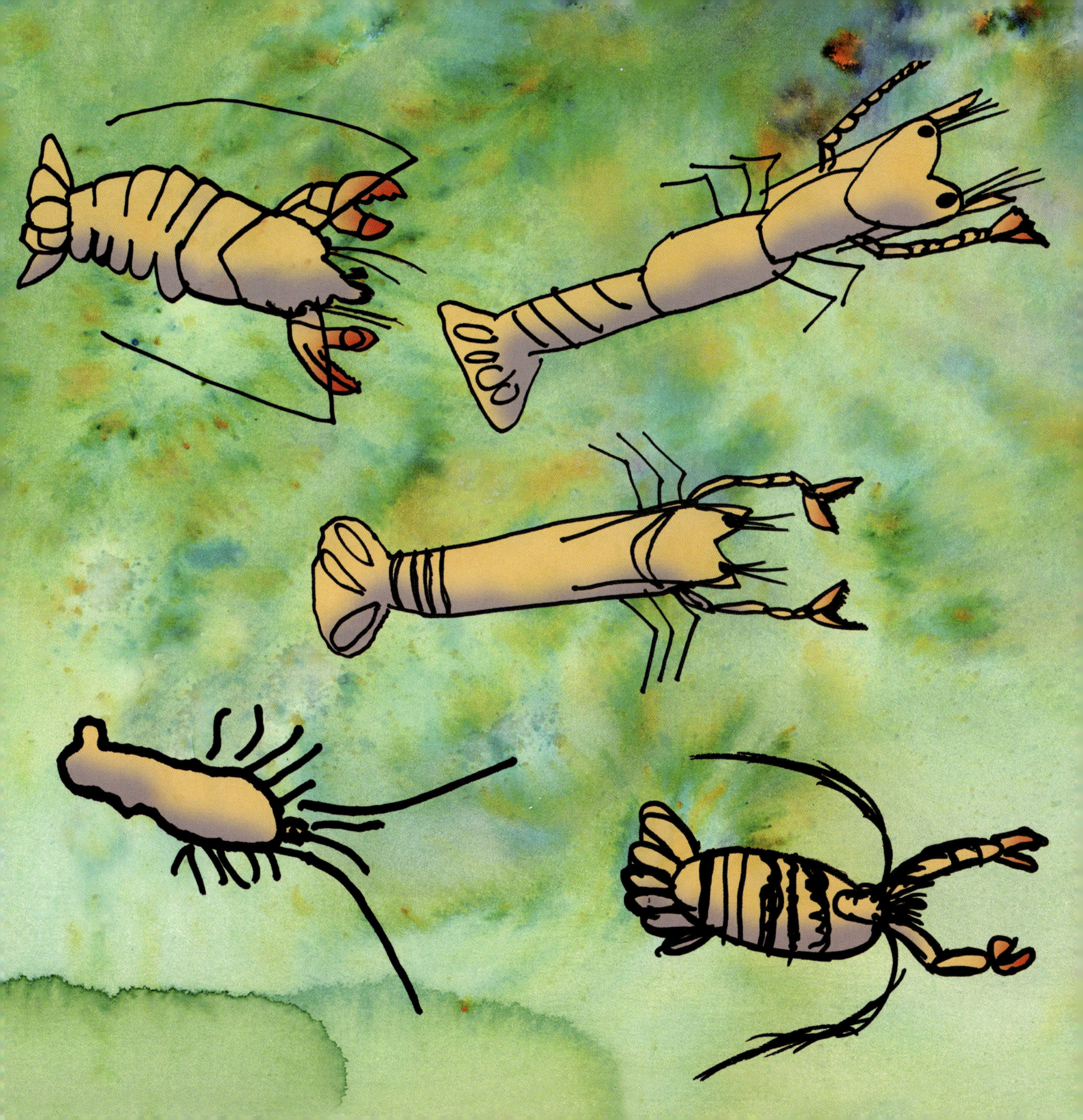

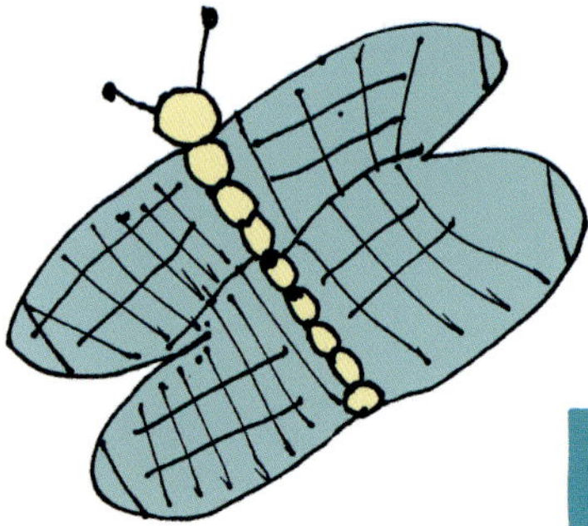

# 10

Waŋgany rulu ga waŋgany rulu

**ḏetj**

buṯthu-buṯthun gurra garramatŋu.

Ten dragonflies, fluttering in the air.

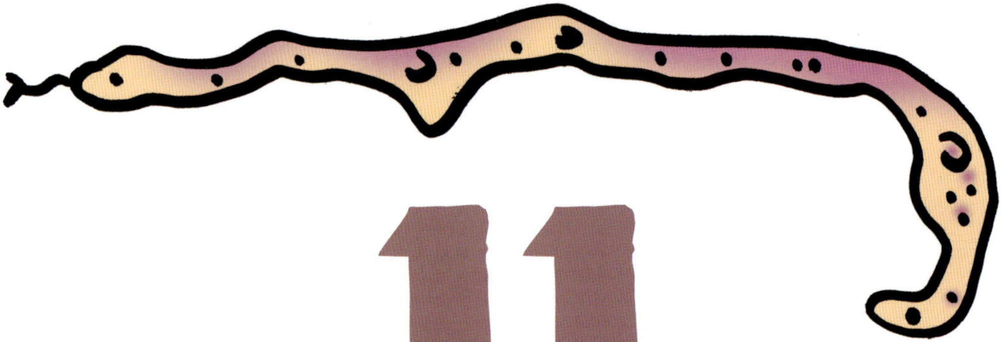

# 11

Märrma' rulu ga waŋgany bäythinyaya

## gapuwuy bäpi

ḻup-ḻupthun gurra mayaŋ'ŋu.

Eleven water snakes, swimming in the river.

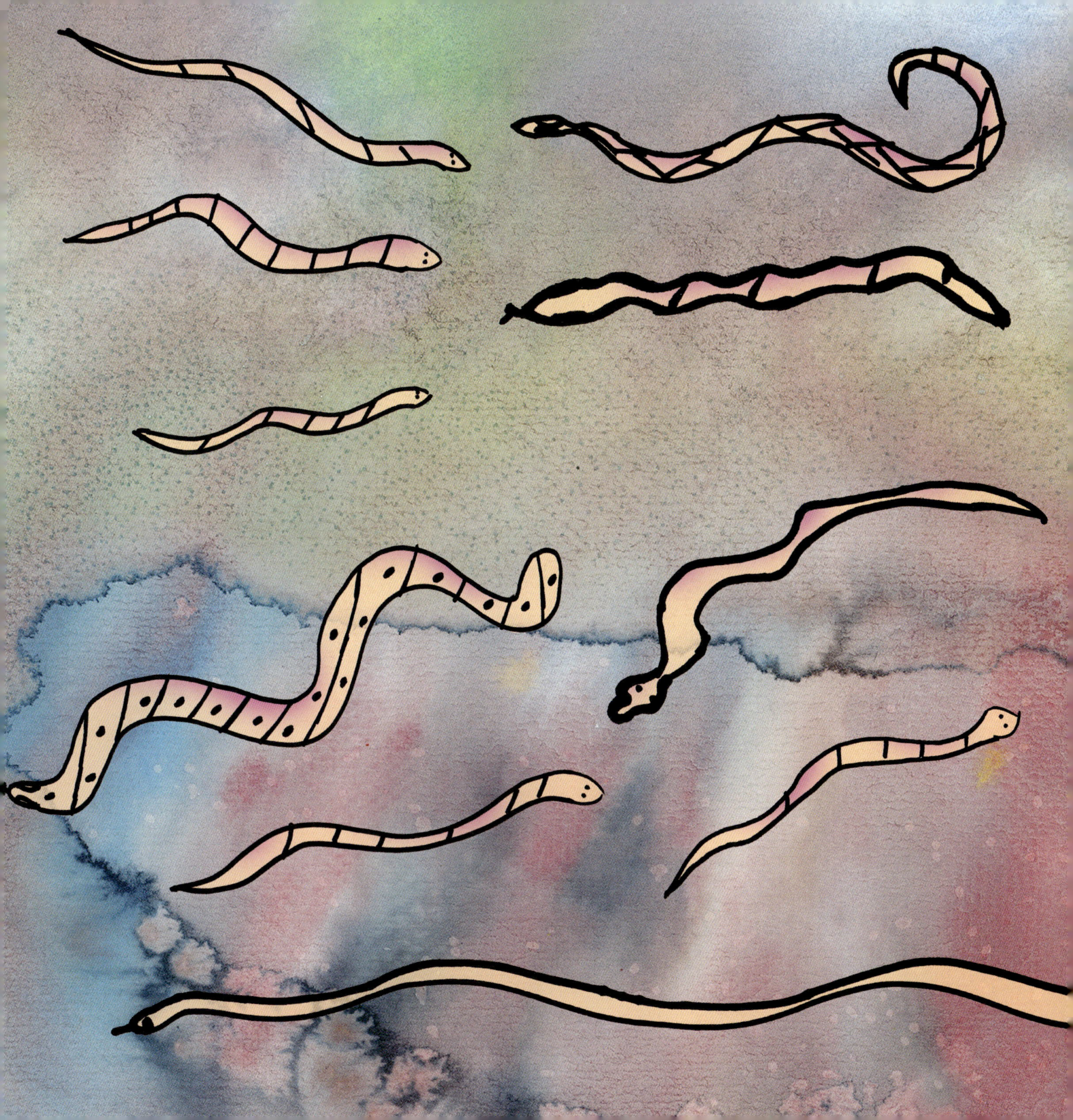

# 12

Märrma' rulu ga märrma' bäythinyaya

## ŋayak-ŋayakmi guya

nhä nhe yurru bothurru bukmakkuma?

Twelve slippery fish – can you count them all?

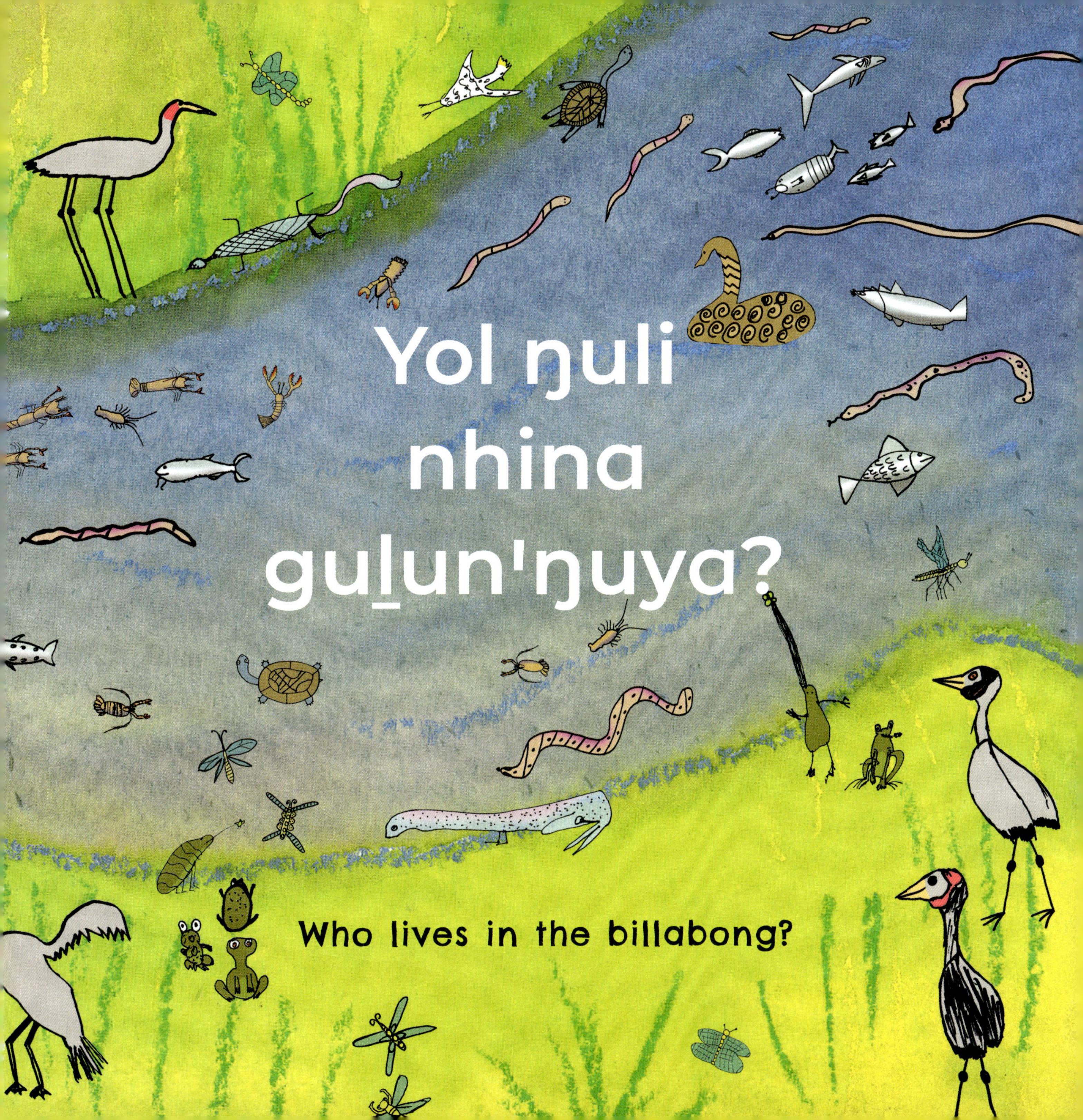

# Yol ŋuli nhina guḻun'ŋuya?

Who lives in the billabong?